THE PHYSICS OF LOVE

THE PHYSICS OF LOVE

Carla Kirchner

Concrete Wolf
Poetry Chapbook Award Series

Copyright © 2017 Carla Kirchner

All rights reserved. No part of this publication may be reproduced, distributed, or transmitted in any form or by any means whatsoever without written permission from the publisher, except in the case of brief excerpts for critical reviews and articles. All inquiries should be addressed to Concrete Wolf.

Poetry
ISBN 978-0-9964754-5-7

Design: Tonya Namura using Minion Pro & Amorie Modella

Cover art:
Mechanical Heart by Margarita Tkachenko/Shutterstock.com
Physics/Mathematics Equations by Marina Sun/Shutterstock.com

Author photo: Kate Kirchner

Concrete Wolf Poetry Chapbook Series

Concrete Wolf
PO Box 445
Tillamook, OR 97141

http://ConcreteWolf.com
ConcreteWolfPress@gmail.com

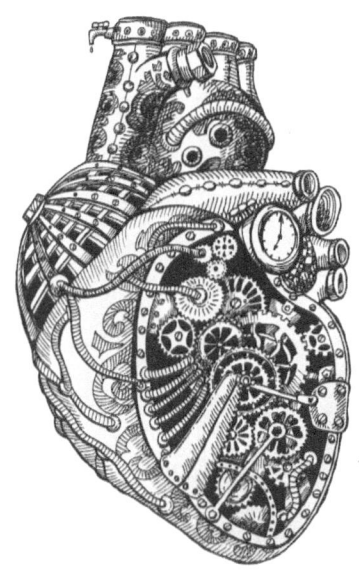

for Roger, Royal, and Naomi

TABLE OF CONTENTS

I. Classical Mechanics

Intrinsic Angular Momentum	5
Motherhood and the Multiple Universe Model	6
Naming the Fire	7
Relativity	9
Ways to Skin a Poem, or The Thursday Night Wild Game Feast at Elk's Lodge #301	10
Newton's 3rd Law	11
String Game Theory	12
A Brief History of Japanese Tattoo	13
The Schrödinger's Cat	14
Boxes	15
Ultraviolet Catastrophe	16
Geology	17
Geometry at the 20-Year Reunion	18

II. Quantums

Simple Machines	21
The Law of Inertia	22
Night On the Mississippi	23
Topography	24
Newton's 2nd Law	25
Gravity	26
Kintsukuroi	27
Laws of Thermodynamics	28
The Fabric of Time and Space	29

The Border Between Heaven and Earth	30
The Uncertainty Principle at the St. Louis Gateway Arch	31
3 More Ways to Skin a Poem	32
The Theory of Everything	33
About the Author	35

THE PHYSICS OF LOVE

1
CLASSICAL MECHANICS

Intrinsic Angular Momentum

I wish I'd been born
with teeth to cut a straight path through
the world instead of this slow spiraling
from my mother. A twisted cord binds me
to earth. Earth circles sun. Sun orbits
the center of the Milky Way. Atoms spin
underneath the skin of everything.

Today they are pushing snow into Boston Bay,
tons of it tumbling with the bluefish
and lobsters. Up north, the glaciers are calving
in the chilly water at the top of the world—
hoary hoof by slimy snout,
the whole mess rolling to the sea.

Forty years ago, my mother studied
the whorls of my fingertips:
I was a snowflake outside her hospital window,
a city wheeling out from its center,
circumference, circular logic,
blood twisting through her heart,
God's round eye.

The moon turned to watch
nurse, nursery, city, snow, mother,
all of us spinning against each other in the dark.

Motherhood and the Multiple Universe Model

We are whole worlds, you and I,
leftover light from violent beginnings,
both of us born of the same big bang.

Two alternate universes, or so the theory goes,
will never be the same. You have my nose
but got your father's eyes, your uncle's tapered fingers.

The collision of two universes leaves cosmic bruises.
You are part of me. Your cells are in my lungs,
kidneys, brain, a parallel planet leaking into mine,
like milk seeping through my blouse.

Naming the Fire

Name him for the place where he was born:
    Bald Ridge, Hardluck Highway, Circus Tent,
    Forked Lightning, Brittle Grass, Heart-of-Pine,
    Grey Smoke, Burning Desire.

Name him after your Great Uncle Fred.
Name him Fire that Destroyed London, that famous
    ancestor now turned to ash.

Name him for what he fears (River, Puddle, Rain).
Name him for what he hopes to be (Wild Devourer
    of Forests, Solitude, Growing Spark).

Name him for destiny and circumstance:
    Boy Born on Cloudy Day,
    Boy Born While Father Was Away,
    Premature, Breach,
    Born in Route, Side of the Road,
    Parking Lot, Back Seat.

Name him prayer:
    This Child will not Die Again, God Did Not Forget
    Me, He Shall Not Get Lost in a Foreign Land,
    Sin-Deny, Mercy and Good Grace.

Forget the baby books with their long lists,
forget the syllables that leap off your tongue or burn
your throat. Already he carries his name into this world
clenched in his tiny fists.

Hurry!—the ceremony is beginning.
Shave his head.

Whisper his name into his ear.
Sprinkle him with gold, grain, valleys,
mansions on hillsides.

It's time to call his soul,
to tie his name around his wrist with silken thread,
to say, *You are My Blessing, My Heart, My Searing Pain,*
The Crimson String That Binds Us,
Red Door Through Which We All Have Come.

Relativity

A mother knows an object shot into space, loosed
from her gravitational pull, moves faster and faster,
ages at an ever-increasing rate.

A child can never fully return.
Inertia always pushes him into adulthood and beyond.

Can it be I wrote this poem only days ago?
(Or was it months? Years?)
Just last week I sent it out into the world, and now
you are reading this while waiting for the 5:15
train or tossing in the strange universe of night when hours
contract to seconds and seconds spiral into infinity.
Now, time is bending verse—
words curl around minutes like restless sheets hug your body.
See! My poem flows like spilt milk through your fingers,
spins like a ball kicked hard to third.
Watch it walk out the door, climb into the bus,
and hurtle away until it disappears.

Ways to Skin a Poem, or The Thursday Night Wild Game Feast at Elk's Lodge #301

For one brief bite, I know the soul of stone and earth,
the secret song the snake sings to the sage grass.
I understand the alligator's scales and all
that is sacred, out of sight, and sweet.

A small boy points to the heart resting on my plate.
"What does it taste like?" he asks.
Like sky, I say, like stars and wind, like the universe
perched at the tip of my tongue.

Newton's 3rd Law

> *"I am an evil genius! I've developed a bomb to blow up the entire consonant."*
> —Royal, age 8

So you want to destroy the world.
First, break *W*'s knees, kick in *R*'s teeth,
shatter *L* into kindling, destroy *D* entirely.
You've seen the films of a building's demise,
how you load its legs with dynamite, blasting cap, fuse,
how the whole thing implodes into its footprint,
    like Grandmother's face sinking through her skull,
    skull falling to hospital bed in a cloud of dust.

But still the *O* remains:
holy vowel, wafer on our tongues,
the curve of Earth's ear. We can't hear our prayers
exploding in the darkness, but they must sound like
soft balls of song, like the rings on our fourth fingers,
like the sound G-d made when He pushed out the World.

String Game Theory

In third grade, I had the whole universe at my fingertips.

I hooked Lightning round my thumbs.
I looped Sea Snake, spread my fingers into Pole Star.
I caught the world inside my Fishnet.
I built a Fence Around a Well and climbed
Jacob's Ladder up to God.

And, if I practiced hard enough, I made The Sunrise.
    I formed Breastbone and Ribs.
        I was Holding Up the Sky.
            I could undo the Moon Between the Mountains
            and shape The World Gone Dark.

A Brief History of Japanese Tattoo

Here, grain towers divide interstate from field.
There are dragons there, my daughter says,
positive of the power stashed in the silos' skin,
so sure the creatures curl up tail to scale,

their breath, the fog on Midwest mornings.
And why can't it be so?—Half a world away,
those dragons curve across the backs of *gokudō*,
whole families pierced with flowers, snakes and god.

It takes years to carve a coat so he can wear
the strength of water; she, the courage of koi.
Irizumi masters know the secret heart of Tokyo
is black with ink and bound with silken thread.

Even now, tattoo must be a hidden art
forced into sleeves and three-piece suits.
We learn to fear what we can't fully see,
all that magic coiled just beneath the surface:

the grocer is an ocean; his neighbor, a tiger;
my own child, a tree bursting into bloom.

The Schrödinger's Cat

is not necessarily dead,
they tell their daughter, who is
made of sensitive stuff, far too

young to meet Grief and Loss.
It's simple to say the cat sleeps
through anything—thunder, sunshine,

radiation mixed with poison—when
they put into a box. It's nice to think
the pet is both alive and dead.

If they lock the cat in a tree with
the neighbor's dog, the cat can
live if no one sees it fall, if no one

hears the sound of canine teeth on
bone and small bowel. It's the same
game their daughter played for days

when she was three, closed her eyes,
and thought herself invisible, breathing
only in the tight box of her brain.

In the dark, it is easy to believe
until she lifts her lids.

Boxes

> *"[A]poem comes right with a click like a closing box."*
> —W.B. Yeats

Your uncle packed the war into a small teak trunk
he bought in Saigon from a girl with empty eyes.
He tries to keep the top on tight, but every night
the screams and bullets spill into his dreams.

This porcelain box does not *click* but *clink*,
the sound of bone on bone.

The small carton marked *happiness* holds her baby teeth,
two 4-H ribbons from the county fair, and a picture of a
duck she drew in third grade. But her *regret* is large
and lidless. She's pushed it deep into her chest,
refuses to unpack it.

A balled sock is a box turned wrong side out.
A cow has four stomachs to hold its food.
Your skull contains your brain.
Your skin hugs your bones.

This morning, I heard the robin throw his box of songs
into the sky. Sky encloses clouds, clouds are full
of lakes, lake is water with parallel sides.
Water is another name for God.

There's a miraculous, four-sided poem in your chest.
You can hear its steady whoosh at night and in the curls
of shells that confine the tide. Listen!—it ebbs
and flows, a box never closed
but never fully open.

Ultraviolet Catastrophe

At thirteen, everything is tragedy—
summer, swimming pools, the cataclysmic
sunburn that left me blistered
and peeled, breathing through my skin.

I was a pause between pollywog and frog,
a comma who'd lost her tail, shedding my skin
day by day. Each night, more and more
of me was lost to the bed sheets or the boredom
of nothing better to do than rip myself to bits
that kept the shape of my shoulders and knees.

I peeled and consumed myself to cover my tracks,
not ready to leave my old life behind
in the grass of the backyard for parents to find.

It was catastrophic work, growing legs and breasts,
learning to live mostly on land with only
occasional swims to remind me of the season
I tested adulthood with my tongue, jumped
back and forth between junior high
and the world of the big pond.

Geology

A rock is a fine profession, if you can get it.

A rock will look you in the eye.
It will fit easily in your pocket and dance when you run.

A rock can be anything it chooses:
sedimentary, foundation, lucky, marble, bridge, house, world.

It's good to be a smooth-souled pebble but better
to be gravel or cave (damp heart still growing),
to be a dark moon in each eye, the stone
at the center of the earth, hidden
beneath fruit and rind.

Geometry at the 20-Year Reunion

In high school,
the list of round things was endless:
suns, oranges, marbles, globes,
all of us rolling blindly into the future.

Gravity squeezed space into planets,
gas merged into stars, entire earths
slipped through God's
giant fingers, smooth as rosary beads.

It's elementary to make perfect ball bearings
in zero-gravity, but on earth you must drop
molten metal into a tube and watch it
settle slowly into a sphere. It's tedious work

requiring wait and patience, which is why
so many of us have flattened into circles,
stretched to squares and triangles, or divided
into straight line segments.

When it was young, the Milky Way was
a tennis ball, too, until it collapsed with age.
Not much naturally has angles, besides
broken rocks, Bob's second marriage,

Susan, Jeffry, Phillip and all of us here
dancing in circles, raising our glasses to 1994
and trying to laugh about all the years, after,
when we became new shapes.

for Neil deGrasse Tyson

11
QUANTUMS

Simple Machines

A pulley pulls
the drive shaft
which spins
the wheels
on their axles
and levers the blade's
inclined plane
through summer
and leaf-fall.

Each morning,
I hose off
my heart,
roll it back in
my chest, and turn
the screw in the lock
so that the World
cannot wedge
his way in.

The Law of Inertia

We are taking the piano apart,
no longer willing to drag it from place to place.
The "A" below middle "C" is stubbornly silent.
I barely remember the lessons or the way
my fingers cupped all that music

Together, we remove the lid.

Together, we heave out its heart and all
its delicate hammers like so many broken fingers.
Each snipped string recoils with regret
until there is nothing left to do but lug it to the curb.

"Perhaps we should keep it," you say.
But how, with all that history between us,
the bench in pieces on the dining room floor,
the keys already scattered to the snow?

Night On the Mississippi

Night measures River's depths.

Her body—upper and lower, divide
    and converge, lock and levee.
Her hands, blue herons against His chest.
Her fluvial fingers.
Her thick brown mouth.

Her breath washes Night in darkness, sucking Him
under before setting Him right, all bruise and splutter,
against the far bank.

She sheds her skin in the dim light:
a blue-black scar flows across Her belly,
reminder of their children now scattered across
the Delta and those summers spent down South, air
so thick and hot He could drown in it
before He even entered the water.

Topography

> *"Terrain features can be learned using the hand to show what each would look like on the ground."*
> —Army Study Guide

When you forget the shape of the world,
you have only to look at your own clenched fist:
its rugged ridgeline, the sloping saddles of your knuckles,
the sheer cliffs on either side of curled fingers
where joy and fear fall into nothingness.
There's a depression inside your cupped palm
or, fingers spread, a valley, all hope emptied to the soil.

Newton's 2nd Law

To the north, the river is crowded with fishermen—
fly fishermen, who keep their own society,
grimly throwing their lines in
and out of the clear water, awaiting
the perfect cast, a fling to heaven
that twists and whips and sings, that slices through the sky
like a prayer. But here on the bridge
my son seems more interested
in reel fishers on slimy rocks
off the bank. They smile and offer him an empty
canvas chair, bright orange dough
for his hook, a pink rubber worm, a handful
of stink bait. They joke and laugh, but even here
fishing is serious business. Pairs of eyes scan the river
for shadows in shallows, for desire moving
through the water. The smallest dreams accelerate
with silver speed. Slower ones hide in the shadow
of the bank. Hope floats just beneath
the surface but rarely takes the hook flung out
by river people who cast and reel, reel and cast all day,
who only live for the first blare of the whistle
and hope to fill stringers before the last blast declares
the fishing day over. Restless, we wander
toward a man cleaning his catch
a few feet downstream. In one cut, the fish opens,
intestines and blood cloud the water
then disappear. The man proudly hands
a breathing trout to my son who reaches for
the shining fish while all around us, up and down
the river, fishermen throw and pull,
in and out, in and out, like breathing. My son
squeals and pokes the pink and black scales, already
running toward the crowded river.

Gravity

> *"Reports of the death of supergravity are exaggerations."*
> —Stephen Hawking

They've taken away Pluto.
San Francisco is lost to fog. I've forgotten
much of what I learned in second grade.

So, it's good to know that gravity (super or otherwise)
is still alive since so many other things are not:
> Dodos. Tasmanian Tigers. Passenger Pigeons. The art
> of letter writing. The salesman who sold my father
> his first single-breasted suit in 1962. Manners
> and Poetry. My father.

Eventually, all bodies seek their natural place.
Tonight, your arms hold me to this room.
My heart is held inside my chest so that when it breaks,
it cannot spin off weakly into space.

Kintsukuroi

When the emperor broke
his favorite bowl, his son melted down his crown
to fill the cracks with gold. A piece of pottery, we're told,
is more beautiful for having been broken.

When Father shattered
into pieces, I glued him back together with my grief.
Now he comes to me in dreams, holding out a coffee mug
patched with fragments of his former life.

The dead always want more.

Nights, he holds out his cup to me and cries his silent pleas:
give me the fillings from your teeth,
the soft sponge in your bones,
try to mend our hearts with gold dust mixed in lacquer,
strengthen the seams that hold us all together.

Laws of Thermodynamics

We can never fully rid ourselves of the dead:

Outside the window, the dead ripen
in the trees before dropping
to earth again and again.

We find their footprints along the fencerows
while navigating the Night Country.

In the Land of Prayer, sister to Sleep, they shed their names
in the short grasses bordering the meadow or leave
their wrinkled skins at the edge of the veiled forest.

And just today, earth steaming with the wee hours
of morning, I saw my father in a Brown-Eyed
Susan by the back door. His body glowed in the faint light.
His voice burnt off the dew with a dense, determined flame.

The Fabric of Time and Space

It seemed like years, the waiting
for Father to pick the perfect suit
while I climbed into racks of wool
and pinstripes. A suit must hang just so,
must be fitting for the Sundays
when he'd open up his mouth
and God would ride out in jockey silks.

It takes hours for silk worms to spool
    out the world, takes 2500 worms to make
        a pound of raw silk, and yards of the stuff
            to line my father's casket.

I've forgotten what suit we buried him in.
I was too busy putting on overalls—snapping
straps, buckling myself together—ready to work
the earth. The world was just beginning to wear
wild onions. The moon traded parka for bathing suit,
placed one leg into night and then the other,
the way apples step into their red dresses and air
makes room for them and for the dogs
in houndstooth, the fish in herringbone.

Angels wear light, cobwebs, fog, and sometimes human faces.
    (They'll spend years in front of mirrors,
    searching their closets for the right coat
    to bring out the color of their eyes
    and that silk tie the shade of the lake
    when it slips into Spring.)

The Border Between Heaven and Earth

is in Bolivia, a flat mirror of water into which clouds dive,
    headfirst,
        then surface with a splutter.

If Heaven and earth are three feet apart,
in the thin places there is even less room to swim
without bumping into God

who sits in puddle, pond, river, ocean,
and in our kiss, soft as sand. Even now, God's name
is in our mouths—*Yahweh, Yahweh*—
a prayer with each breath, both of us beaches
breathing in the dark.

The Uncertainty Principle at the St. Louis Gateway Arch

I count it a small miracle the five of us can hunch
into the egg-shaped elevator and take it to the top,
uncomfortably nestled in the opening
to East and West, Above and Beneath,
Impossibility and Existence.

How wondrous this monument straddling two worlds!
How amazing this precarious ride, so like our first one,
when hesitant, unnamed, unfixed in time and space,
we travelled to earth curled in heaven's womb
and waited for the doors to open.

3 More Ways to Skin a Poem

The family to the south slaughters a sow.
On Friday night, they shoot her right above the eyes,
slit her throat, let her bleed, a sacrifice to sky and leaves.
At dawn, they scald, carve,
    render,
        eat.
(Your neighbors to the north do not eat pork,
but each Friday at dusk they kill the lights.
Mother's *Shabbat* prayers open Heaven's door,
pool on the floor beneath her feet. Saturday,
they chew on Yahweh: sweet shoulder of morning,
belly of the afternoon, the evening's firm, round rump.)

You can still remember summers
Grandma tied a rooster to the clothesline by his feet,
severed its red head with one quick sweep.
Something left in him still flapped its wings—
Amen, Amen, Amen, again *Amen.*

We all have decisions we must make.
Brisket or ground beef? Stew or London Broil?
You can't have both fillet and porterhouse.
Will you keep the heart, liver, or tongue?
Oh Lord, let every tongue confess! the preacher cries
each Sunday when he opens God and serves Him rare,
still warm: His ribcage, His Grace, His flank and shank,
His enduring Mercy, His firm right hand,
His awesome hanging weight.

The Theory of Everything

The house where God lives
is made of glass and sits by the sea.
Inside are a round table with three chairs,
jugs of wine (their numbers multiplied each evening),
bowls filled with furred globes of fruit.
There is a leather couch the color of mist
and a quilt made from the afterbirth of galaxies.

Seven doves perch in seven golden cages.
Five cats clean their paws of night and shadow.
Two Cocker Spaniels fetch the bright ball of morning
or, come dusk, its pale, sad twin.

Because God likes to feel the beach beneath His feet,
at dawn He digs for clams and numbers every grain
of sand, each shell, and all the longing
littering the shore.

After lunch, He unties His skiff and rows out past
the edge of the world before rowing back again.

Come darkness, He wraps himself in cloud and listens
to our evening prayers, our voices blending with the surf.

Through His picture window, God watches us bob
in the water. "Hello, hello!" we wave:
    up and down,
        in and out,
            crest and trough,
                an eternal tide of humanity.
And He smiles and waves back.

ABOUT THE AUTHOR

Carla Kirchner lives in the Missouri Ozarks. She holds an MFA in Creative Writing from Spalding University and writes both poetry and fiction. Her poetic prose, flash fiction, and short stories have recently appeared in *Literary Orphans, Rappahannock Review, Eunoia Review, Foliate Oak Literary Magazine, Gravel,* and *Unbroken Journal.* She is currently at work on a collection of Civil War fairy tales and a series of poems about her grandmother's Kentucky girlhood.